I am Not Married to a
Bottle of Wine
Part- 2 reunion

Poems in
(english, portuguese, french, italian, kimbundu, chinese and spanish)

written by
A.D.I (f.faria)

First Published in December 2020

ISBN: 978-93-5427-041-3

BLUEROSE PUBLISHERS
www.bluerosepublishers.com
info@bluerosepublishers.com
+91 8882 898 898

Cover Design:
Mohd Arif

Typographic Design:
Ayushi Garg

Distributed by: BlueRose, Amazon, Flipkart

Contents

Honey Moon / 1

Lets not Wait Till Love Runs Dry / 2

Fever / 4

Knives Falling and Raining / 5

Im a Christian / 7

Automatic / 8

His Wishes / 9

Two Girls / 10

Psalm 91 / 11

The Green Leaves / 13

Betrayal / 14

Psalm 91 / 15

Small Funny World / 17

Please Change / 18

We Did / 20

Three Trees / 23

She has a Mark / 24

The Recipe Book / 26

Turn the Page / 28

My Childhood Pictures / 30

Marathon of Life / 32

Embraces in the Snow / 34

Waterfall Shower / 36

Growing up but Never Finding / 38

No songs on the Radio / 39

Poems / 40

I'm not Married to a Bottle of Wine / 41

Love No More / 43

Two Days After the End of the World / 46

2 Dias Depois Do Fim Do Mundo (Portuguese) / 47

Meu Amor (Portuguese) / 49

Eternel (French) Eternal / 50

Fuego (Spanish) / 51

Voglio (Italian) / 52

HUA (Chinese) Flower / 53

Hua (Translation)Chinese / 55

Mona (Kimbundu) / 58

Bestseller / 59

Honey Moon

I won't dim the light of your eyes

Will have your eye lit with chandeliers and candles

I even imprisoned a star and wrestled a lion to take u on a honeymoon

Nectar pollen and honeysuckle a pillow made of pollen I'll light up the sky with candles that burn with glitter

I know heaven is made with love so I wanted to marry. You from the moment I met you and I began walking without touching the ground floating in romance as we married and my ring was a golden diamond

First. Baby was immaculate conception in our sight newlyweds just married hallelujah Jesus for. Gifting me with her

Lets not Wait
Till Love Runs Dry

Let's not wait until the well dries

Let's not fall into this abysm

Will end our relationship before its too late

Well at least we remain friends

I will remember the good times

Let's not wait until love runs dry

Let's just say goodbye

When there are no more words to say

When conversation has ended

Let's not wait for that

Let's break up fresh and nicely

Let's break up beautifully

Let's have the sweetest break up ever

Let's not wait for disaster

Let's not wait for destruction

Let's not wait for erosion

We will break up with gifts and smiles

Let's end up smiling and loving

Let's dream our break up and make it real

Let's have an easy break up.

A digestible break up

A happy ever after break up

I'm Not Married to a Bottle of Wine

Fever

We were young
We had fever to live
We had fever to run
We used to run without limits
We crossed borders
We jumped hills
Over the fence
We crossed neighbourhoods
We stole pineapples from the corner shop
We had stupid fever
We did not sleep
We thought we would conquer the globe
We dreamt to be rich
We had fever
We thought we were better than everybody else
We had fever
We use to party all night
We use to look for girls
We had stamina
We had fever

F. Faria

Knives Falling
and Raining

It was raining knives

It was raining bullets

It was raining swords

It was dripping blades

It was raining stones

It was raining blood

It was raining fire

It was hell

It was pure hell

It was just hell

Could it be a meteor falling next?

It was raining knives again

Could it be an UFO

Worst than bombs

Worst than atomic power

The world falling

It Was raining mountains

It was raining trees

It was raining cars

A twister may be was happening

It was raining dinosaurs

I'm Not Married to a Bottle of Wine

Im a Christian

Had to tithe

Had to sacrifice my body

Had to deny me

Prayed to be saved

Prayed for repentance

I'm a Christian I'm a spiritual soldier

Life is about spiritual warfare

I'm a Christian

I'm a follower of Christ

Had to go to church

Had to read the bible

Had to follow the principles

Prayed for every thing

I'm he who he loves most

Im precious in heaven and despised on earth

I'm a Christian

I'm everything for the angels

They are even more to me

F. Faria

Automatic

Nowadays everything is automatic

I'm lazy about getting up

The alarm is automatic

I'm lazy about cooking

The toaster is automatic

I'm lazy about eating this is not automatic

I'm lazy about watching TV

The remote is automatic

I'm lazy about walking out

Well

The car is automatic

I don't have to open the door

The door is automatic

I'm lazy by convenience

I'm lazy about talking

The answer machine is automatic

The globe in automatic

The gadgets

The machinery

The automatic is ruling

I'm Not Married to a Bottle of Wine

His Wishes

My wishes are wild
Like animals in a jungle
I knew we had to tangle
She was very humble
Her beauty was different
His wishes were of possession
He wanted to have more
Dreamed about getting down
Walking south
His wishes
Were never like hers
His wishes were like this
A little dark a little white
To embrace and caress
Just one caress
He was her favourite suitor
His wishes became hers
They just held hands
It started with a wish

Two Girls

They went to church
Two girls had future in their hands
Two girls read their prayer
They cleaned the house
They were obedient to their parents
They were responsible for shores
They listened to their mother
Two girls that were hard workers
From birth they were taught respect and values
Morals they memorized
Two girls would conquer the globe
School work done always on time
Always the best students of their class
Two girls that reminisced greatness
Two girls
Were the pride of the city
Earned all the accolades
Remained humble throughout
Graduated with honours
Married virgin
Two examples
Too good to be true
F. Faria

Psalm 91

1

Whoever dwells in the shelter of the Most High
will rest in the shadow of the Almighty.[a]

2

I will say of the Lord, "He is my refuge and my
fortress,

my God, in whom I trust."

3

Surely he will save you
from the fowler's snare
and from the deadly pestilence.

4

He will cover you with his feathers,
and under his wings you will find refuge;
his faithfulness will be your shield and rampart.

5

You will not fear the terror of night,
nor the arrow that flies by day,

6

nor the pestilence that stalks in the darkness,
nor the plague that destroys at midday.

7
A thousand may fall at your side,
ten thousand at your right hand,
but it will not come near you.
8
You will only observe with your eyes
and see the punishment of the wicked.

The Green Leaves

The air that we inhale

The breath that we take

We exhale this air

This air I need

Coming from this green leaves

Coming as a gift from the almighty

The green leaves are precious

The leaves fall

They grow they renew

The green leaves are treasure

Plant another tree

Don't end up like Amazon

We need the forests

We need the green spaces

We need parks

We can't just have buildings

The air we need

Could not live without

I'm Not Married to a Bottle of Wine

Betrayal

My best friend betrayed me

Betrayal hurts more than stabbing

I never ignored you

I never did wrong to you

Your betrayal was cruel

Betrayal with the one I love

I don't know which betrayal hurt most

Which one of you did worst

Betrayal hurts more than death

Betrayal is death

Death of our friendship

Because of betrayal

Death of trust

Due to betrayal

Death of hope

Came with betrayal

Betrayal is worse than a slap

A slap on the face

Betrayal is a slap on the face

I'm Not Married to a Bottle of Wine

Psalm 91

If you say, "The Lord is my refuge,"

and you make the Most High your dwelling,

10

no harm will overtake you,

no disaster will come near your tent.

11

For he will command his angels concerning you

to guard you in all your ways;

12

they will lift you up in their hands,

so that you will not strike your foot against a stone.

13

You will tread on the lion and the cobra;

you will trample the great lion and the serpent.

14

"Because he[b] loves me," says the Lord, "I will rescue him;

I will protect him, for he acknowledges my name.

15

He will call on me, and I will answer him;

I will be with him in trouble,

I will deliver him and honor him.

16
With long life I will satisfy him
and show him my salvation."
13

Small Funny World

If walls could talk

You would know I don't lie

At times I feel distant

Away from the globe into the stratosphere

The atmosphere is like a sphere

Round and limited

Boundaries and limitation between us

With you beside I feel fulfilled

We all look for a reason to live

Not to throw tears in vain

Not to cry without a reason

Crying out of season

In the desert of loneliness

Amidst bushes and bees

To throw tears in vain

At times is best to cry for somebody

Instead of crying for nobody

Have somebody to cry for

It is a small, funny world

You just look and you will agree

F. Faria

Please Change

Change the way you dress

Don't say the same things

Please change

Please, please, please

Don't take me to the same places

Everyday eating the same food

At the same table

Please change

Hanging around with the same people

At the same time

Saying the same jokes

Please change

Please, please, please

Drinking from the same cup

Watching the same TV program

Besides god

Don't want you to be the same

Need you to change

Tell me a different lie

At least try

Don't change the same change

Go to China for a change

Change your history

F. Faria

We Did

We did tangle

We did hug

We did make love

When we held hands I heard a rumble

Heard a bark and a laughter

All the words I did mumble

I whisper carelessly

I whispered loudly just for her ear

That's how we became lovers

She was very humble

We did almost get lost

Into a stumble

In out footsteps

Waling in our shoes

You won't like our path

I was trying to fumble

We were together for a meal

Dinner was before lunch

Breakfast was before lunch

We did kiss for lunch

Breakfast was strawberry

Bought blueberry too

A cherry

We did do it done

We done doing it we did it

I'm Not Married to a Bottle of Wine

The suitcase of my age file

The important man

Carrying a suitcase

A therapist

With my psychological profile

Telling me who I was

The diseases and thoughts

How long I was to live too

All in a suitcase

All inside a file

With estimates

How much I was to spent

In my lifetime

How much I was to love

In my lifetime

He had it in a file

All my credit card purchases

All my adresses and friends

The 666 day

He looked unusual

Knew all my family tree by heart

He knew me better than I knew myself

F. Faria

Three Trees

Neighbourhood was an issue in the
neighbourhood

Noise and commotion

People talked loudly

The secret to peace

Staying together with whom you love

If you don't wanna lose your girl

Take her to apicnic under the three trees

Before her coffee break

Take her for manicure afterwards

Pedicure is a must

Always have some candy handy

To avoid the neighbourhood madness

Noise in the city

Chaos behind the skyscrapers

The cement on the road

The mechanical heat

The exhaust fumes

The secret to peace

Was to stay under the three trees

Paint your house orange too

I'm Not Married to a Bottle of Wine

She has a Mark

She had a very distinct mark

On her forearm

Near the armpits

She had a mole

Not a beauty one

She had a mark

Maybe in her heart

She had the mark of deception

The history of broken houses

The memory of bad relationships

She carries a mark

Everywhere she goes there is the mark

You may not see it

There is a clear mark

Wrinkles and blisters

Blisters are wrinkled

She has a mark

Of suffering

Beating and abuse

Well he also has a mark

She is not alone

He suffers as well

He has a mark deeper than hers

I'm Not Married to a Bottle of Wine

The Recipe Book

My grandmothers cook book

It had all the recipes

From generations back

All the secrets

Written in peppermint and cucumbers

Inked with tomatoes and onions

The recipe book as we knew it

My grandfather knew nothing about it

He only ate

He never divorced her because of the food

Some say that is why he married her

The recipe book

It took a hundred years to gather

Our great greats started it

We will have to finish it

The secrets of our generational stomach health is there

We were blessed by liver

Gifted with good stomachs

The secrets were in the recipe book

Our DNA our IQ

All in one recipe book

Was folded in a basement

Coiled with aluminum

I'm Not Married to a Bottle of Wine

Turn the Page

Turn the page from yesterday

Move on from your past

Challenge what the future holds

Passerby may count your tears

But you have to move on

Stay together

Turn the page

Past is gone

Become a newborn person

A baby adult

Read the books like a new person

Today is a dream

Yesterday a ray of light was beaming

Detours are occasional

Roller skate past yesterday

Release your worst fears

Let your inhibitions aside

Turn the page

A new chapter unfolds

Finish the book

Encyclopedia of pain

Turn over the page

My Childhood Pictures

They were gathered in an album

My childhood pictures

My hair was so weird

My childhood pictures were motive of laughter

Summer cousins came

We always looked at them

Some went missing

My most valued possession was my baby
photograph

Coats hanging as visitors came in

Bell was ringing well before we opened

Before the food

We saw the pictures

I tore the most embarrassing ones

The same scene

Someone telling me they cleaned me as a baby

Saw me cheat myself

My childhood pictures were embarrassing

Me an almost father being disrespected

In front of my own fiancé

My childhood pictures were me

I could not hide from them

I'm Not Married to a Bottle of Wine

Marathon of Life

Run the marathon

100 meters race

Marathon of life is much worse

You can be fast

She can be strong

No one is sure to cross the line

The marathon of life

Being in front

Doesn't secure being the first to cross the line

The marathon of life

Is a bumpy road

Hurdles to jump over

Pace yourself

When you get to heaven

You may get to hell

All here on earth

The marathon of life is challenging

Be a daredevil to finish it

Some are winners others are losers

Afford to be saved to get to the finish line

See you when you get to heaven

Say your prayers and be righteous

The marathon of life3

It is really tough

F. Faria

Embraces in the Snow

It was dripping cold outside

We gave embraces in the warm snow

Our body temperatures were double glazing

Heat was contained

Time was stopped

The globe stopped spinning

The stars stood still

The moment the moon took a picture

Captive eyes of strangers

Birds were tearful

Embraces in the snow

Waterfalls and Cinderella fountains

Candy rain and sugar sky

Strawberry lips

Ice cream skin

Embraces in the snow were cool

A cool warmth

A warmth cooler than ice

Ice icy and vanilla ice

Embraces in the snow

Avalanche of feelings

The two of us under moonlight

Candlelit sky

Starlit eyes

I'm Not Married to a Bottle of Wine

Waterfall Shower

Waterfall shower

In the jungle

That is how we rolled

Ocean baths

Waterfalls shower

We were balling out of control

Nature knowing

Walking bare feet

Bears and lions and monkeys

Banana catching

We were having the fun

We were the meaning of fun in the dictionary

Taking waterfall shower

Water coming down from heaven

River washing our hands

We were playing Adam and Eve

Romeo and Juliet

Me and her

I was Tarzan

Sometimes Chaka Zulu

We were gladiators

Crocodile hunting avoiding

Swimming with the mermaids

Growing up but Never Finding

I thought when I grew old
I would find answers
Growing up was easy
I'm taller
I'm not sure if I am wiser
Growing up was boring
Now I want to regress
I thought I would progress
Growing up was easy
But I ended up never finding
What I looked for
What was I looking for?
Getting closer to death
I want to start again
Be a child again
Be a toddler again
Take me back in time
Let me live the movie again
Growing up and never maturing
I'm still a child at heart
Growing old
I'm Not Married to a Bottle of Wine

No Songs on the Radio

Today there will be no songs on the radio

No songs playing

Musicians are on strike

No songs no melodies no poems

No poets

Musicians are poets

No piano, no strings, no drums

No songs on the air waves

No songs on the radio

No songs to be heard

No singer alive

No keyboard and no board

No radio and not a Walkman

No iPod and no mp3

No songs on the radio

No songs to touch lovers

No songs on the dance floor

Sad parties and unhappy birthdays

I'm Not Married to a Bottle of Wine

Poems

Poems are lonely

Poems are in the soul

They tell the truth

Poems are solid in our being

They tell a story

They move mountains

Like faith a poem is a source

It can give you hope

It can make the world spin

Because without it

There would be no journey

Poems change life

Journey in a word

Poem in a mouth

Poems are simple

Poems are complicated

I'm Not Married to a Bottle of Wine

I'm not Married to a Bottle of Wine

When I walked down the altar

I never thought my vows were to a bottle

I never knew I was going to spend my life getting drunk

Drunk by the smell

Drunk by consent

just like passive smoking I was getting passive drinking

I was never sober

I was either drunk or in the middle of it

I know exactly how it feels

To feel like a glass of wine

That is how I felt every time you touched me

Now in alcoholic anonymous meetings I swear divorce

I want divorce from the bottle of wine

The package looks good

The content says only ten per cent alcohol

Drink chilled with peppers for supper

But I know that's a lie

Because 100 per cent of the time its alcohol

There's no water in this bottle

I know it from the kisses

The swerving behaviour the confused speech

The uncoordinated walk the lack of sobriety

I married a bottle of wine

Or did I just consent to living with one

Even when its whisky

It still feels like wine to me

My surname is…………

Well you guessed it

Produced in France or Portugal that is your fame

Your package is excellent

But marriage with you is a disgrace

Love No More

love no more

I love you no more my dear

Not that I hate you

I just don't love you this year

Its surely not love like before was lovely

I fear there is only one tear left

And there no running water in the tap of my eye

I love you no more than hatred

I want you no more yet I seek you

Far too many times you used me

Far too often I used you

You were inside of me taxing my runway

I was inside of you the port of whatever

To my soul I say I love you no more

In spirit I say to my body

I love no more I landed on sorrow

No more I hate you I travelled to anguish

You are so far away

You left me for dead

You were unfaithful to my orders

I was not feeling what I thought

I was not thinking what I felt

The body betrayed the mind

So its love no more
I'm Not Married to a Bottle of Wine

IM NOT ME

I'm not me anymore

Will I find myself

At sunset of dawn

Through the signs of another day to moan

Will I remember me one day

Time has changed me

Near the sunrise I hid a pearl

Only I know the place

Near my heart I have all my secrets hidden

For there are hours that last years

Some years last only minutes

At the blink of an eye I reason about time

Will I be me tomorrow?

In space I get lost

Trying to find myself through the whirlwind

Caved in uncertainty

A tornado of feelings arose

A waterspout drowned my only hope

I'm not who I was

I'm not me he is not me

We are the same but we are not

I have changed, climbed barbwire in life

Went down an abyss

Rapture that took me over

In past I was who im no longer

Will I find myself?

Do I know who I was?

My childhood was buried

My childhood me is dead

I have grown bitter

I don't recognize myself.

Two Days After
the End of the World

Hey neighbor

Stranger

Today you greet and grim

Many times we don't speak

I wish i could borrow salt

Work home work

Our kids don't even play

You stroll past my sidewalk

Only in emergency we know each other

Even something as easy as saying.hello

Birthday parties pregnancies

Seems we only unite in tragedy

Jesus wants us to love.one another

Mortgages likes preferences are trivial

2 Dias Depois Do Fim Do Mundo
(Portuguese)

Quando o vírus passar

Es

uma pessoa muito rara e tens um espaço guardado
no meu coração

Meus

sentimentos em quarentena a espera que tu
venhas me

libertar

Quando o vírus da solidão passar seremos livres
para nos amar com

o unico

antídoto para tristeza separação e solidão que e' o
amor puro que reservo para ti e por ti

tao

puro ele e' que e' bebível e um sentimento quase
comestível como gomo sem semente ou voo de
uma pomba sem rajadas de ar quando penso em ti
e nesse amor que será eterno e o foi antes de se
consumar Basta um encontro para

selarmos nossa

aliança os anjos aguardam em antecipação da celebração que será o dia que eliminarmos o vírus da distância e separação um olhar verdadeiro um sorriso sincero e uma alegria

de alivio jesus amem.

Meu Amor (Portuguese)

Meu amor não e' escola

Meu amor não e' batismo

Mas sim ruelas que se perdem num beco sem
saída

E os beijos são piramides do

Egipto com oásis e camelos desenhados em areia

movediça.

Meu Amor não e' filme

Meu amor não e' livro.

Mas sim rascunho

De uma porcão exagerada de magnifico

E numa cabaça furada aguá a gotejar

Melaço nas minhas palavras não são algodão-doçe
nem chocolate.

Meu amor e" Prova

Professora paixão bom dia

Sou euzinho teu aluno

Apaixonandose me segura

Antes que seja tarde demais.

Escrito por(o poeta invisível) edicao limitada (
turma dos bonecos)jesus. Gracas amem

Eternel (French) Eternal

La lumiere dans vos yeux

La lumiere de dieu

L'eternel Jesus

Je regarde toi

Insistentment

Je suis amoureux

Parle mois

Avec la lumiere dans vos coeurs

Fuego (Spanish)

fuego en tus ojos

oír tu voz

mil veces amor

el dolor

partiste ayer

fuego en mi corazón

el espirito santo

mi condena

fuego di amor

háblame

adonde estas

fuego y amor

mujer cristiana

Voglio (Italian)

trovo nel tuo

occhio

una rosa per favore

dire

dove sta

el amore

per te faccio

tutto la amicizia

voglio amarle

buongiorno ne la mattina

buongiorno ne la notte

amor mio

la mia preghiera

voglio amare

come el figlio de dio gesu

amo a noi tutti

un bacio eterno

Africano

HUA (Chinese) Flower

Hua

接着，我为大家朗诵一首我自己写的诗

花
她叫花
请再说你的名字一遍
花
在我的甜蜜蜜的梦我已经认识你
她是红色和绿色
许多颜色我不清楚
有朋友的颜色， 有爱的颜色

花
她叫花
就像最好的点心
在孩子的生日给他们绿色的花
因为孩子的梦没有绿色的云
我看红色的雨， 我看花
花要水
水要风

在我的梦我看花一遍

我在暖和的公园认识你

天气冷， 她也微笑

花

你的名字短

她叫漂亮叶

你的眼睛开始下雨

花， 请不要在花瓶睡觉

花能说

花能睡

睡在我的心

我有她的照片在我心

基督

HUA (Translation)Chinese

Hua

Flower

Ta Jiao Hua

She Is Called Flower

Qingwen Zai Shuo Nide Mingzi Yibian

Please Your Name Again

Hua

Flower

Zai Wode Tianmimi De Meng Wo Yijing Renshi Ni

In My Swetest Dream I Already Know You

Ta Shi Hongse He Luse

You Are Red And Blue

Duo Yanse Wo Bu Zhidao Qingchu

Many Colors I Dont Know

You Pengyou De Yanse Gen Ai De Yanse

Friendship Color Love Color

Hua Ta Jiao Hua

Flower She Is Called Flower

Yiyang Wode Zuihao Dianxin

Like My Best Dessert

Zai Haizi D E Shengri Gei Nimem Lu Yanse De Hua

In Childrens Dreams Give Them Blue Flower

Yinwei Haixi De Banye Meng Meiyou Luse De Yun

Because Childrens Dream Have No Blue Clouds

Wo Kan Hong Yanse De Xiayu Wo Kan Hua

I Saw Red Color Rain I Saw A Flower

Zai Feng Zai Hai Wo Yong Hua

In The Wind In The Sea I Need Flower

Hua Yong Shui

Flower Need Water

Shui Yong Feng

Water Need Wind

Zai Wode Meng Wo Kan Hua Yibian

In My Dream I Saw Flower Again

Wo Renshi Ni Zai Nuannuo Gongyuan Hua

I Know You In The Warm Park Flower

Zhengzai Ta Weixiao Yiwai Hai Leng Tianqi Hua

While She Smiled It Was Also Cold Flower

Nide Mingzi Nuan

Your Name Is Short

Ta Jiao Piaoliangye

You Are Called Beautiful Leaf

Nide Yanjing Kaishi Xiayu

Your Eyes Start To Rain

Hua Ta Bu Suexiao Zai Huaping

Flower You Dnt Sleep In A Flower Pot

Hua Neng Shuo

Flower Can Talk

Hua Neng Shuejiao

Flower Can Sleep

Shujiao Zai Wode Xin Wo You Tade Zhaopiao Zai Wode Gennao

I Sleep In My Hear

I Have Your Picture In My Brain

Jesus Jī Dū Christ

Mona (Kimbundu)

Mona ya dyala

Eme dijina kidi

Mona ya yesu

Mu bibidya

Izwelu ikola mu kimene

Eme dijina lelu

Mona ya nzambi

Mu Cabinda

Eme mona ya nekulu

Angola Ixi ye

Afrika mam'etu.

Bestseller

1 Im Not Married To A Bottle of Wine,

2 Ultimate Shortcut 2 Heaven

3. Last Virgin of The World, Boyfriend Girlfriend
   Dating Doesnt Exist

ADI.WRITERS

F.FARIA

Ixi Yetu Mandume

Fidel Passos

Valdemiro Carlos

Gloria Etelvina

oaspc2@hotmail.com

Few Mad Crew Supervision

Reunion

Project world family

Quick facts

Mona means son, African language kimbundu

Fuego means fire Spanish

Eternel means eternal French

Voglio want in Italian

Printed in the USA
CPSIA information can be obtained
at www.ICGtesting.com
LVHW012353050424
776610LV00011B/292